KENTUCKY

Julie Murray

VISIT US AT
www.abdopublishing.com

Published by ABDO Publishing Company, PO Box 398166, Minneapolis, MN 55439.

Copyright © 2013 by Abdo Consulting Group, Inc. International copyrights reserved in all countries. No part of this book may be reproduced in any form without written permission from the publisher. Big Buddy Books™ is a trademark and logo of ABDO Publishing Company.

Printed in the United States of America, North Mankato, Minnesota.
042012
092012

 PRINTED ON RECYCLED PAPER

Coordinating Series Editor: Rochelle Baltzer
Editor: Sarah Tieck
Contributing Editors: Megan M. Gunderson, BreAnn Rumsch, Marcia Zappa
Graphic Design: Adam Craven
Cover Photograph: *iStockphoto*: ©iStockphoto.com/wsfurlan.
Interior Photographs/Illustrations: *AP Photo*: AP Photo (p. 23), Cal Sport Media via AP Images (p. 27), Michael Conroy, File (p. 21), Frank Franklin II (p. 25), Dan Grossi (p. 25), North Wind Picture Archives via AP Images (p. 13), stf (p. 21); *Getty Images*: Adam Jones/Photo Researchers (p. 5); *Glow Images*: Superstock (p. 27); *iStockphoto*: ©iStockphoto.com/BasieB (p. 30), ©iStockphoto.com/lillisphotography (p. 26), ©iStockphoto.com/visionsofmaine (p. 11); *Shutterstock*: Martynova Anna (p. 30), Stephen Bailey (p. 29), Steve Byland (p. 30), Anne Kitzman (pp. 9, 19), krechet (p. 26), Phillip Lange (p. 30), Christina Richards (p. 19), Henryk Sadura (p. 11), Alexey Stiop (p. 17), Todd Taulman (p. 27), traxlergirl (p. 9).

All population figures taken from the 2010 US census.

Library of Congress Cataloging-in-Publication Data

Murray, Julie, 1969-
  Kentucky / Julie Murray.
      p. cm. -- (Explore the United States)
  ISBN 978-1-61783-355-7
  1. Kentucky--Juvenile literature. I. Title.
  F451.3.M875 2013
  976.9--dc23
                    2012005981

KENTUCKY

Contents

One Nation

The United States is a **diverse** country. It has farmland, cities, coasts, and mountains. Its people come from many different backgrounds. And, its history covers more than 200 years.

Today the country includes 50 states. Kentucky is one of these states. Let's learn more about Kentucky and its story!

Did You Know?

Kentucky became a state on June 1, 1792. It was the fifteenth state to join the nation.

4

Cumberland Gap is a famous mountain pass in southeastern Kentucky.

5

KENTUCKY UP CLOSE

The United States has four main **regions**. Kentucky is in the South.

Kentucky shares its borders with seven other states. Tennessee is south. Missouri is west. Illinois, Indiana, and Ohio are north. West Virginia and Virginia are east.

Kentucky's total area is 40,411 square miles (104,664 sq km). About 4.3 million people live in the state.

REGIONS OF THE UNITED STATES

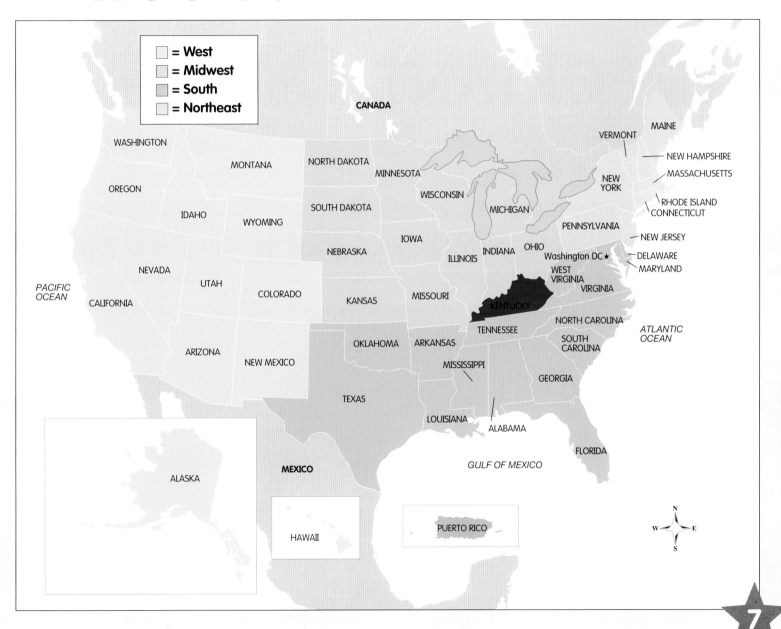

= West
= Midwest
= South
= Northeast

CANADA

WASHINGTON

MONTANA

NORTH DAKOTA

MINNESOTA

VERMONT

MAINE

NEW HAMPSHIRE

MASSACHUSETTS

OREGON

IDAHO

WYOMING

SOUTH DAKOTA

WISCONSIN

MICHIGAN

NEW YORK

RHODE ISLAND

CONNECTICUT

PENNSYLVANIA

NEW JERSEY

IOWA

NEBRASKA

ILLINOIS

INDIANA

OHIO

Washington DC ★

DELAWARE

MARYLAND

NEVADA

UTAH

COLORADO

KANSAS

MISSOURI

WEST VIRGINIA

VIRGINIA

PACIFIC OCEAN

CALIFORNIA

KENTUCKY

NORTH CAROLINA

ATLANTIC OCEAN

ARIZONA

NEW MEXICO

OKLAHOMA

ARKANSAS

TENNESSEE

SOUTH CAROLINA

MISSISSIPPI

GEORGIA

TEXAS

LOUISIANA

ALABAMA

FLORIDA

MEXICO

GULF OF MEXICO

ALASKA

HAWAII

PUERTO RICO

N
W   E
S

7

IMPORTANT CITIES

Frankfort is the **capital** of Kentucky. It is located on the Kentucky River. About 25,500 people live there. That makes it one of the smallest US capitals.

Louisville (LOO-ih-vihl) is Kentucky's largest city. Its population is 597,337. Many goods are shipped from its airport and river port. The city is also known for hosting the Kentucky Derby.

Kentucky

Louisville • Frankfort ★ • Lexington

• Bowling Green

N W E S

★★★★★★★★★★★★★★★★★★★★★★★★
The current Kentucky State Capitol was built in the early 1900s. It is the state's fourth capitol building since 1792.

★★★★★★★★★★★★★★★★★★★
Louisville sits across the Ohio River from the state of Indiana.

Lexington is Kentucky's second-largest city. It is home to 295,803 people. It is known for its beauty. The area has rich soil and fields of bluegrass. Also, the University of Kentucky is located there.

The state's third-largest city is Bowling Green. Its population is 58,067. It is home to important businesses. Chevrolet Corvette cars are one of many products made there!

Major businesses are based in Lexington.

Many horses are raised on farms near Lexington. This city is known as "the Horse Capital of the World."

11

Kentucky in History

Kentucky's history includes Native Americans, explorers, and settlers. Native Americans hunted and farmed in present-day Kentucky for thousands of years.

In 1776, Kentucky became part of the Virginia Colony. As settlers arrived in the 1770s, Native Americans fought for their land. Many people died during this time. Still, settlers worked hard to build towns. Kentucky became the fifteenth state in 1792.

Daniel Boone was a famous pioneer. He visited Kentucky for the first time in 1767. Later, he began a settlement there called Boonesborough.

13

Timeline

1750

Virginia doctor Thomas Walker led a group of explorers to Kentucky. He discovered the Cumberland Gap.

1792

Kentucky became the fifteenth state on June 1.

1875

Horses raced for the first time at the Kentucky Derby in Louisville.

1700s

1800s

Harrodstown was founded. This later became known as Harrodsburg. It is the oldest town in Kentucky.

The **American Civil War** began. Some people from Kentucky fought for the South. But more fought for the North.

1861

1774

1956

Restaurant owner Harland Sanders founded Kentucky Fried Chicken. Over time, it grew into a popular chain of fast-food restaurants.

2010

The story of racehorse Secretariat became a popular Disney movie. This real-life horse famously won the Triple Crown in 1973.

1900s

2000s

A special building was completed at **Fort** Knox to store US gold.

Martha Layne Collins became the first female governor of Kentucky.

1936

1983

ACROSS THE LAND

Kentucky has **grasslands**, mountains, and forests. It is famous for its wide fields of bluegrass. And, the Appalachian Mountains run through the southeastern part of the state.

Many types of animals make their homes in Kentucky. These include woodchucks, bats, and wild turkeys. Rivers and lakes are home to many types of fish.

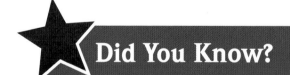

Did You Know?

In July, the average temperature in Kentucky is 77°F (25°C). In January, it is 34°F (1°C).

Cumberland Falls is one of Kentucky's natural wonders. People often visit Cumberland Falls State Resort Park.

17

Earning a Living

Kentucky is a manufacturing and service state. Businesses there make cars, food, and **appliances**. Many people work for the state and local governments. Others work at the state's major military **forts**.

Kentucky's land provides the United States with important products. Mines provide coal. Farms produce a variety of crops.

Did You Know?

Louisville and Lexington form the "Golden Triangle" with nearby Cincinnati, Ohio. This area is where most of Kentucky's people and businesses are found.

The coal from Kentucky's mines helps provide electricity for the United States.

Tobacco and corn are two of Kentucky's important crops.

Sports Page

Many people think of horses when they think of Kentucky. This state raises many racehorses. And, it has been home to a famous horse race called the Kentucky Derby since 1875.

The Kentucky Derby is one of three important races called the Triple Crown. The derby is held every May at Churchill Downs in Louisville. Thousands of people attend. Before the big race there are fireworks, parties, concerts, and a parade.

Around 150,000 people attend the derby each year. Millions more around the world watch it on television!

In 1973, a racehorse named Secretariat became famous. He was one of only a few horses to win all three races in the Triple Crown!

HOMETOWN HEROES

Many famous people are from Kentucky. Country singer Loretta Lynn was born in Butcher Hollow in 1935. She often wrote songs about her life. Her first song came out in 1960.

In 1980, Lynn wrote a book called *Coal Miner's Daughter*. It tells the story of her life. Lynn grew up poor in Kentucky. But, she followed her dreams and became "the Queen of Country."

Did You Know?

Lynn became a member of the Grand Ole Opry in 1962. This is a big honor for a country singer.

In 1978, Lynn was honored with a star on Hollywood's Walk of Fame.

23

Famous boxer Muhammad Ali was born in Louisville in 1942. In 1960, Ali won a gold medal at the Summer Olympics. He went on to become the heavyweight boxing champion three different times!

Ali is also known for standing up for his beliefs. He refused to fight in the **Vietnam War** even though that was against the law.

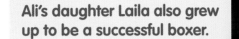
★★★★★★★★★★★★★★★★★★★★★★★★★
Ali's daughter Laila also grew up to be a successful boxer.

★★★★★★★★★★★★★★★★★★★★★★★★★
Ali's given name was Cassius Clay. In 1964, he changed it because of his religious beliefs.

25

Tour Book

Do you want to go to Kentucky? If you visit the state, here are some places to go and things to do!

 ## ★ See

Visit a horse farm in Lexington. You can see horses eat and run in grassy fields.

 ## Taste

Have some fried chicken at the Harland Sanders Café in Corbin. This is where Kentucky Fried Chicken began. You can also see some items from the restaurant's beginnings.

Cheer

Catch an exciting college basketball game! The University of Louisville Cardinals and the University of Kentucky Wildcats are popular teams.

Remember

Visit Abraham Lincoln's birthplace near Hodgenville. There's a one-room log cabin like the one his family lived in.

 Explore

Tour Mammoth Cave. This is the longest cave system in the world! You can also hike, camp, or canoe in Mammoth Cave National Park.

A Great State

The story of Kentucky is important to the United States. The people and places that make up this state offer something special to the country. Together with all the states, Kentucky helps make the United States great.

Kentucky's white-fenced horse farms are world famous.

Fast Facts

Date of Statehood:
June 1, 1792

Population (rank):
4,339,367
(26th most-populated state)

Total Area (rank):
40,411 square miles
(37th largest state)

Motto:
"United We Stand, Divided
We Fall"

Nickname:
Bluegrass State

State Capital:
Frankfort

Flag:

Flower: Goldenrod

Postal Abbreviation:
KY

Tree: Tulip Tree

Bird: Northern Cardinal

30

Important Words

American Civil War the war between the Northern and Southern states from 1861 to 1865.

appliance a machine for the home, such as a refrigerator, that is powered by electricity.

capital a city where government leaders meet.

diverse made up of things that are different from each other.

fort a building with strong walls to guard against enemies.

grassland a large area of grass, with little or no trees.

region a large part of a country that is different from other parts.

Vietnam War a war that took place between South Vietnam and North Vietnam from 1957 to 1975. The United States was involved in this war for many years.

Web Sites

To learn more about Kentucky, visit ABDO Publishing Company online. Web sites about Kentucky are featured on our Book Links page. These links are routinely monitored and updated to provide the most current information available.

www.abdopublishing.com

Index